❀ GIRLS ❀

COLORING BOOKS

DETAILED DESIGNS VOL 1

▲ ART THERAPY COLORING

Preview of Coloring Pages

www.arttherapycoloring.com

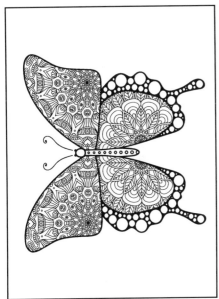

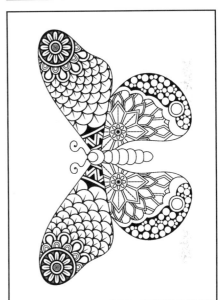

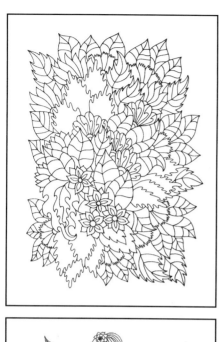

Did You Enjoy Our Coloring Book?

We Want To Hear About It!

Help spread the word about our adult coloring books! We give 10% of all proceeds from Art Therapy products to benefit pancreatic cancer patients and their families.

The best way to spread the word is through reviews. We know how busy you are, especially with all of that coloring, but we would appreciate it!

Visit our website at **www.arttherapycoloring.com**

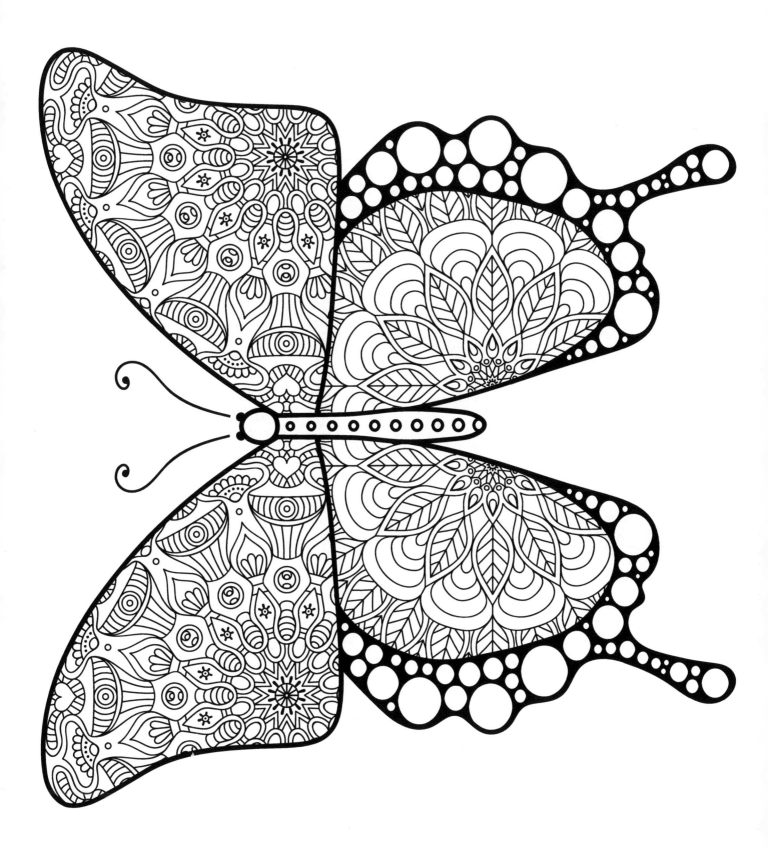

Visit our website at www.arttherapycoloring.com

Get a Free Printable Coloring Ebook!

We've created an exclusive offer for our customers to receive a free Adult Coloring Ebook.

Visit **www.arttherapycoloring.com/freebie** to claim your free coloring book with over 30 new designs that you can instantly print and color!

Over 100 Art Therapy Coloring Books

See our collection of over 100 Art Therapy Coloring Books for Adults, Men, Seniors, Teens, Kids, Boys, and Girls on the following pages.

Coloring Books For Girls

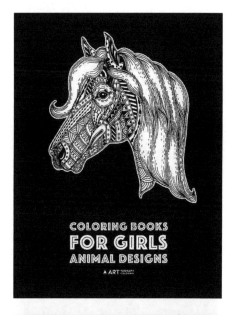

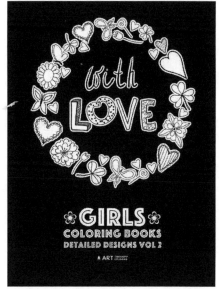

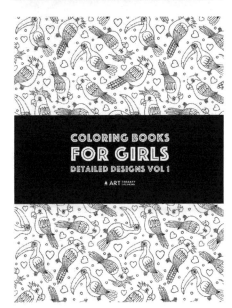

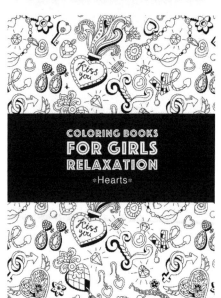

Coloring Books For Boys

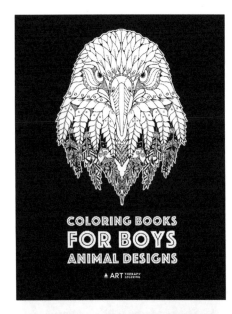

COLORING BOOKS
FOR BOYS
ANIMAL DESIGNS
ART THERAPY COLORING

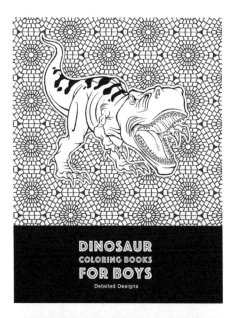

DINOSAUR
COLORING BOOKS
FOR BOYS
Detailed Designs

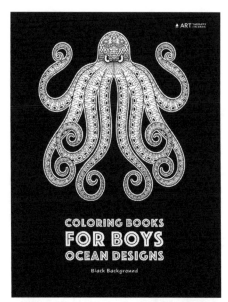

COLORING BOOKS
FOR BOYS
OCEAN DESIGNS
Black Background

COLORING BOOKS
FOR BOYS
NATIVE AMERICAN INSPIRED
ART THERAPY COLORING

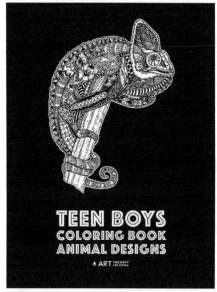

TEEN BOYS
COLORING BOOK
ANIMAL DESIGNS
ART THERAPY COLORING

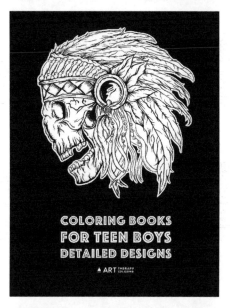

COLORING BOOKS
FOR TEEN BOYS
DETAILED DESIGNS
ART THERAPY COLORING

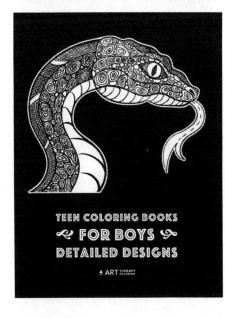

TEEN COLORING BOOKS
FOR BOYS
DETAILED DESIGNS
ART THERAPY COLORING

COLORING BOOKS
FOR TEEN BOYS
DETAILED DESIGNS
Black Background

TEEN COLORING BOOKS
FOR BOYS
DETAILED DESIGNS
Black Background

Coloring Books For Kids

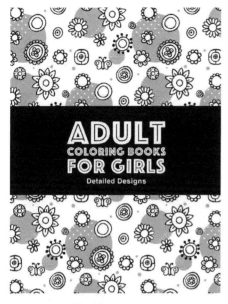

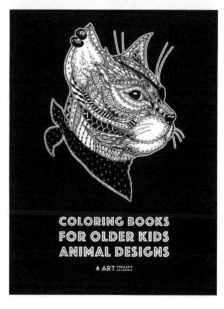

Coloring Books For Teens

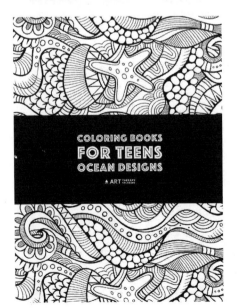

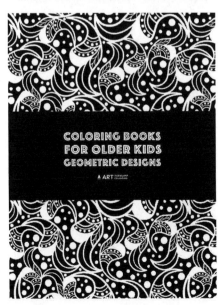

Coloring Books For Teens

COLORING BOOKS FOR TEENS RELAXATION
Nature Designs

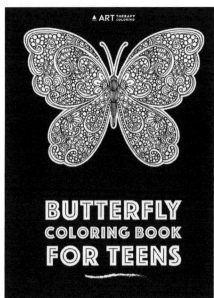

BUTTERFLY COLORING BOOK FOR TEENS

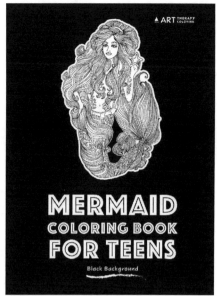

MERMAID COLORING BOOK FOR TEENS
Black Background

ANIMAL COLORING BOOK FOR TEENS VOL 2

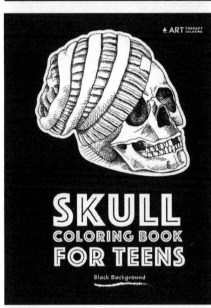

SKULL COLORING BOOK FOR TEENS
Black Background

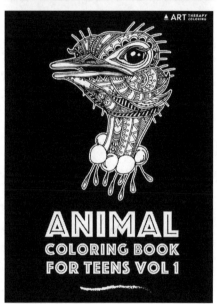

ANIMAL COLORING BOOK FOR TEENS VOL 1

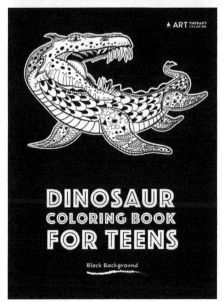

DINOSAUR COLORING BOOK FOR TEENS
Black Background

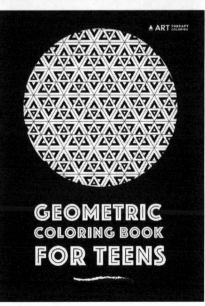

GEOMETRIC COLORING BOOK FOR TEENS

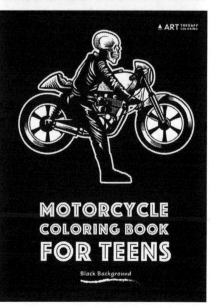

MOTORCYCLE COLORING BOOK FOR TEENS
Black Background

Coloring Books For Teens

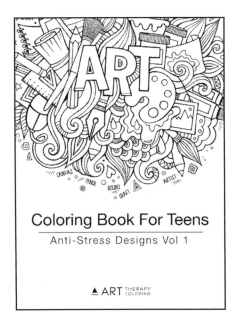

Coloring Book For Teens
Anti-Stress Designs Vol 1

▲ ART THERAPY COLORING

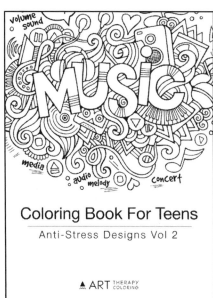

Coloring Book For Teens
Anti-Stress Designs Vol 2

▲ ART THERAPY COLORING

Coloring Book For Teens
Anti-Stress Designs Vol 3

▲ ART THERAPY COLORING

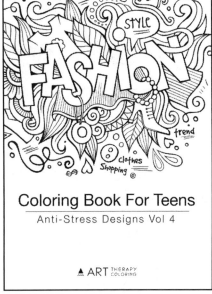

Coloring Book For Teens
Anti-Stress Designs Vol 4

▲ ART THERAPY COLORING

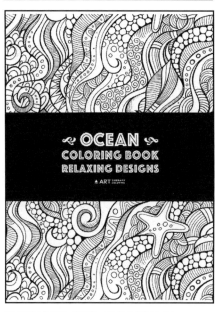

Coloring Book For Teens
Anti-Stress Designs Vol 5

▲ ART THERAPY COLORING

Coloring Book For Teens
Anti-Stress Designs Vol 6

▲ ART THERAPY COLORING

Coloring Book For Teens
Anti-Stress Designs Vol 7

▲ ART THERAPY COLORING

Coloring Book For Teens
Anti-Stress Designs Vol 8

▲ ART THERAPY COLORING

Coloring Books For Men

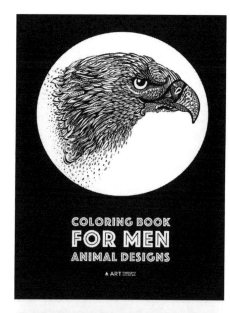

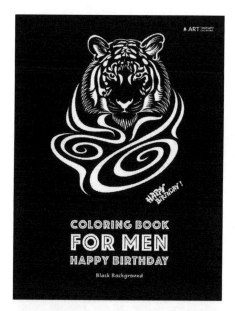

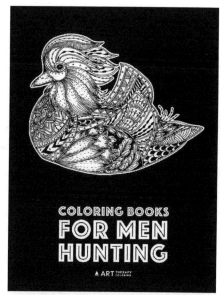

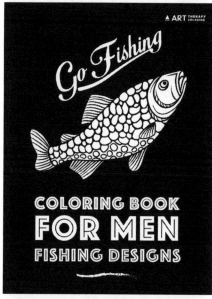

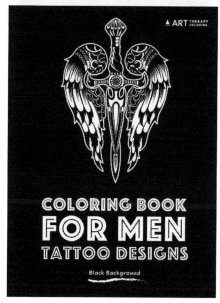

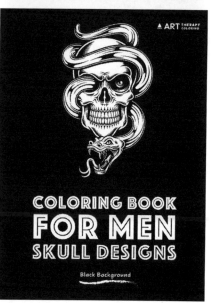

Coloring Books For Adults

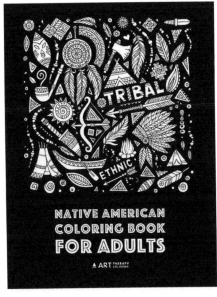

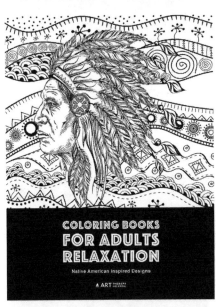

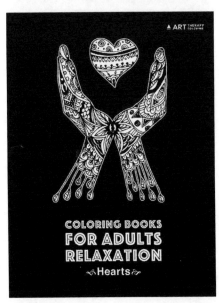

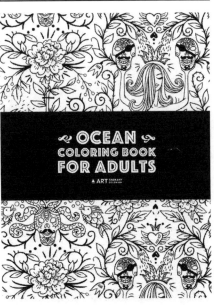

Coloring Books For Adults

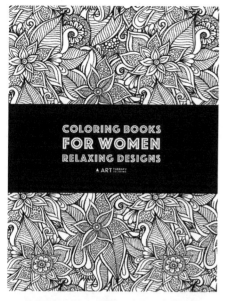

COLORING BOOKS
FOR WOMEN
RELAXING DESIGNS
ART THERAPY COLORING

COLORING BOOKS
FOR GROWN-UPS
RELAXING DESIGNS
ART THERAPY COLORING

COLORING BOOKS
FOR RELAXATION
ANTI-STRESS DESIGNS
ART THERAPY COLORING

OWL
COLORING BOOK
FOR ADULTS
ART THERAPY COLORING

SWIRLS
COLORING BOOK
RELAXING DESIGNS

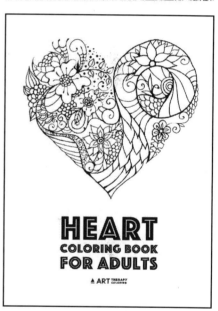

HEART
COLORING BOOK
FOR ADULTS
ART THERAPY COLORING

LION
COLORING BOOK
FOR ADULTS
ART THERAPY COLORING

WOLF
COLORING BOOK
FOR ADULTS
ART THERAPY COLORING

TIGER
COLORING BOOK
FOR ADULTS
ART THERAPY COLORING

Coloring Books For Seniors

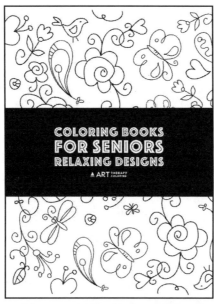

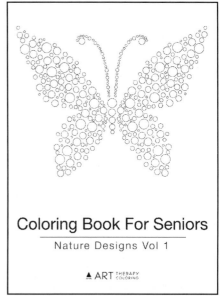

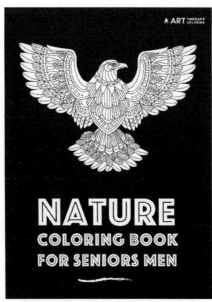

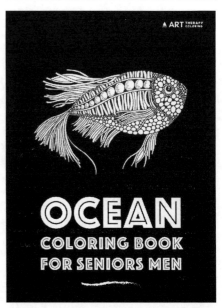

Coloring Books For Special Occasions

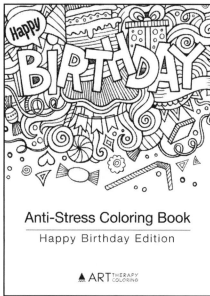

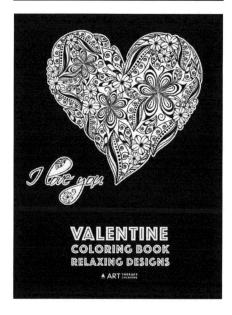

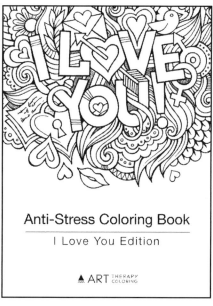

Coloring Books For Christmas

Girls Coloring Books
Detailed Designs Vol 1

Published by:
Art Therapy Coloring
El Dorado Hills, California
www.arttherapycoloring.com

Shutterstock Images

ISBN: 978-1-64126-041-1

Made in the USA
San Bernardino, CA
29 August 2018